BOA
EDITIONS
LIMITED

T0131404

BRIGHT HUNGER

Bright Hunger

Poems by

MARK IRWIN

AMERICAN POETS CONTINUUM SERIES, NO. 83

BOA Editions, Ltd. — Rochester, NY — 2004

09 10 11 12   5 4 3 2

Publications by BOA Editions, Ltd.—
a not-for-profit corporation under section 501 (c) (3)
of the United States Internal Revenue Code—
are made possible with the assistance of grants from
the Literature Program of the New York State Council on the Arts,
the Literature Program of the National Endowment for the Arts,
the Sonia Raiziss Giop Charitable Foundation,
the Lannan Foundation,
as well as from the Mary S. Mulligan Charitable Trust,
the County of Monroe, NY,
the Rochester Area Community Foundation,
Ames-Amzalak Memorial Trust,
and The CIRE Foundation.

See Colophon on page 88 for special individual acknowledgments.

Cover Design: Daphne Poulin-Stofer
Cover Photograph: "Ancient Wasp" by Walt Saeuger, courtesy of the National Park
    Service, United States Department of the Interior.
Interior Design and Composition: Richard Foerster
Manufacturing: United Graphics
BOA Logo: Mirko

Library of Congress Cataloging-in-Publication Data

Irwin, Mark, 1953–
    Bright hunger : poems / by Mark Irwin.— 1st ed.
        p. cm. — (American poets continuum series ; v. 83)
    ISBN 1–929918–52–6 (pbk. : alk. paper)
    I. Title. II. Series.

PS3559.R95B75 2004
    811'.54—dc22

                                                            2004000360

NATIONAL
ENDOWMENT
FOR THE ARTS

NYSCA

BOA Editions, Ltd.
Nora A. Jones, Executive Director/Publisher
Thom Ward, Editor/Production
Peter Conners, Editor/Marketing
Glenn William, BOA Board Chair
A. Poulin, Jr. Founder (1938 – 1996)
250 North Goodman Street, Suite 306
Rochester, NY 14607
www.boaeditions.org

CONTENTS

I

II

III

IV

. . . animate
The trivial days and ram them with the sun . . .

—W.B. Yeats, "Vacillation"

for Mary Lou Irwin
& for Lisa Utrata

I

SONG

—To whistle once into a forever wind.

And the light from the sky pooled around us.

We put our hands into it and rubbed it on others, ones distant
or gone.

And chance assigned us a time, and our bodies grew.

And we became aware, then our bodies grew tired, and our minds
were taken away.

Yes, some of us have been found, but what's lost
often remains forever.

Sometimes in the middle of October an April occurs, and we marvel
at green bursting through the papery yellow,
then it snows and the sun comes out all across the white page.

And you stand there, dusted in a brightness, moving alone.

A GLASS OF WATER

The stars, for the glimpsing,
for the gazing beyond. A crush of stars
heavy with the dark October sky.

Or red blood cells scattered on the slide's white
field. Worlds without, worlds within.

Yesterday, in the tall grass
by a creek below mountains and forming
mountains of cloud, there was
nothing I wanted to possess, I who love
the flesh so much and try to make
a house within poems.

When my clumsy hand first learned to write *yes*
I placed a sun over trees by a river
and realized much later
yes cannot be written. And *no* is a stone growing larger
until it shrinks, finally unnoticed
within the mountain.

Petru sang in the choir in Bucharest, sang in the choir
as a boy, and later worked as a barber in Auschwitz
where his jaw and teeth were broken.

Now he sells auto parts in Cleveland. He says
radiator and wipes the spit from his chin.
Marina, he says, *her name was Marina.*

Pour a glass of water in sunlight. Now lift
it toward your mouth and try to imagine
the same act in a fleshless world.

The sky's swarming with stars. To sing
nothing into being. Grass, trees,
and clouds. Just try.

PASSING

It is now   this late evening in April
among first irises and bees I realize
they were opening doors   Mary   Robert
and William   I want to say of clouds   sunlight
rain now   Didn't we notice the arrows
of hearts   hands   leaping toward an unmapped
when   No age no place though all of one
light   Somewhere beneath that cloud
in a little town   a white door is opening
maybe for nothing but wind   but we will all
one day be there   I mean when opening is finally enough

———

AN AUTUMN ESSAY

Everything happens at once, a world sifting its yellow
leaves to sing a lessening sun. The tulle wrapped around
the goldenrod and pupa
like a veil only found in cloudish

ways. On TV Sister Wendy spoke of Botticelli—
his name means little barrel. He stole
gold leaf to paint Venus' hair. And while Sister Wendy
spoke, Lisa's caterpillars hung from each of several

stems. Their larval bodies were beginning to change
as the first snow dusted the mountains—a fire
in us that said "go there." Someone we knew
was dying. He drove a silver Corvette for hundreds

of miles to watch the stars. His long white hair
blew in the wind while a monarch caterpillar
hung from a thread. Its green body
would swell and mummify to some pellucid

capsule, clearer and beyond, till one morning
we noticed the inlaid gold beads haloed
about the crown, and then—barely visible—
the apricot, yellow, and black-striped

wings. Plato came to mind as I drove to see
my white-haired friend. We went fishing
at Monument Lake, and when the trout hit the elk
caddis, I knew it lessened the pain, just as the snow-capped

mountains and his mistress from Texas did.
She cooked fried green tomatoes with bacon and
trout. Another friend opened hundred-dollar bottles
of wine. We smoked cigars and looked at the stars. No one

asked about the pain, but we remembered
the lake and fish. Everyone agreed it was the best
meal we'd ever had. We got drunk.
We danced. We turned the ranch upside down

and Joe forgot for a while as we
walked long into the night and he talked of his family.
I remember he had a dog named Rocket,
dead now, but boys still call its name.

—•—

BECAUSE

in that country we live only a day, how
slow the hours of each season. How we find
in each lingering now all moments
just as you once found in the cloud
of death one leaf of joy, and in that leaf
a rain of laughter within which lay
one hidden scream, unflowered. And while

in the spring of one morning a woman
watches tulips open and thinks of a man,
if you were to enlarge her invisible reach
you might see along the skin of her arms
thousands of tiny dice, and within

the black marks of each die, the turning
stars. And if you were to tape the birdsong
of that country, then play it back at an
infinitely slower speed, you would hear
within each silver chirp something like
the wheels of an enormous train rushing
toward an ocean you can't see but smell.

MEMORY

Sunlight, shade, sunlight.
Earth of her, earth of him. Love, when we dig
with our heads like a pig for all that is edible and good.

She was a river through him and he was a river through her,
while the fire in each moved toward the other, the fire that was an
     orange
sea. They were swimmers to orange while the world shrank
all around, but in that world he remembers the green

ring she had given him. Once in April, hidden among spirea,
they made love outside and he was stung by a bee.

His hand became swollen and they had to cut the ring.
They had been drinking gin and he still remembers his finger in the
     vice
and them laughing as she worked the hacksaw across the gold band.

And what of those sentences fleshed with emotion and the future
they spoke to one another?

That's just geography, a black unflesh of words refusing to be eaten by
     earth.

He remembers the sting now as a kind pain.
Years and seasons and the bloated sun rises over a green world.

And somewhere above the pencil's grey noise it's raining and the sun
is out and I'm thinking, as the heat rises to make a little wind, how exact
the sadness is, yet how generous and inextinguishable the joy.

———

OF A LONG INSTANT

All these moving bodies, so many bodies moving
toward some where, some when. I think chance lies in motion,
truth in the wind we feel. And years later how impossible they're gone,
yet how possible these flowers, cuffed where they walked, reached,
and finally touched, smelling into another world. In between
there's love, a kind of marvelous glue holding things
in place, at least for a while. So we sat down at the enormous
table, and as we spoke years crept from the wine's bouquet,
an invisible traffic, redolent of summers, and voices,
some yellow and joyous, some purpling with an inexplicable
sadness, and then it was snowing and we could not

move. The white page is like that, bracing in its grip, bracing
in its stare till the insect words begin to move, mate, producing
the ghost larvae always feeding on emotions until they
become words, or a sentence crawling toward some flight
all its own. In spring I have seen the words swarm
upon a loved one, wiggling their tails, humming
toward or beyond all meaning. I guess it doesn't matter, just so
the glue holds. And when it doesn't, or we get older, there's always
God. I think about him, the small word a cloud whose light
strikes us dumb. I believe something in all that vanishes and in
vanishing reminds of that closer, tiny flame each instant

blames on the sweaty air. The *is* is what's constantly
slipping away, but shocking us occasionally all the way
from where we didn't notice. But to create one moment
so sensuously ecstatic that it destroys time. Wouldn't
that be the wildest of all affections? She's blowing
out the candles, your daughter, and now kissing the boy
in the dark kitchen, and the photograph, fading, goes
on holding the winded flames, tiny sunsets, spring
dandelions, laughter, then children—hers—standing over
your grave. And someone who was there still smells
smoke, the frosting. Yes, evenings will call as we grow

older till it seems the very doors pass us by. Nature
helps some—I think—for there it was a green world
undid my mind. I planted seeds, fed cows, horses,
wandered through fields wearing a coat of light, listening
to the speech of grasses, content I thought as were
all animals till I watched a porcupine for hours
circle, sniffing slowly, pawing another that didn't
move—a bundle of sticks—as the gap grew longer
and the one, living, ambled away, carrying an enormous
misunderstanding in its black eyes. A funeral
for one, once, lingering only awhile, as a breeze lingers.

Look, over there, faces you love are already bronzing
in a faraway light that goes and is gone, losses
you can never absorb, till grief is the sound of a hissing
river, or a fire remembering green. But radiantly
lost the dead return, moving blindly through our memories,
tripping occasionally on some palpable joy that dissolves
like ice in a boy's hot hands. But to know
the immeasurable animal hours, the duskflower of each lake
nodding on its stem, and the stars, glimmering in their veil
—yes's farther side—is to know patience's slow wheel, a mouth
that grazes, bellowing in the air, while I hurried just enough
so that motion would fan the entirely beautiful blaze of my destruction

waiting for the not-so-insignificant wind of me. Was it then
I realized that happiness is a kind of puzzle, and while
some arrive completely, others stumble into a room, carrying
a few extra pieces in their hands? Were they the planners,
scribbling names in datebooks, while millions of bacteria
squatted beneath their thumbnails, new roguish civilizations
waiting to touch or be touched? I prefer watching this
tiny red spider forge new territory across a blank
white page, hoping it will detain me from some terrible
event I will never see unfold, or perhaps teach me
something about intention without attachment and the surrendering
of words to a whiteness beyond this wishful here.

NOVEMBER

Now across the fields there's a wall of gold,

and evenings, if you listen closely enough,

there are faint horn and trumpet sounds.

It's the sun moving through grass

reflecting toward cloud, as the buttery

light of the straw says, "Lay

me down." A boy, invisible to most, is

carrying a plate of brass toward you.

Font of what? And you would like to fill

your pockets with a glow blurring all

specifics with its shine. Hurry, please,

for the boy's growing older. Look, already

there are wrinkles on his hands, around

his eyes. He would like to give you

what you will never entirely have. And

what is that ringing you can feel?

—•—

FUSE

Most of what I do or read does

not help me understand what is

always going. I turn and the *was*

gets bigger, a blanket that has

covered many: I see bodies

kindle as they pass; their voices

hiss to nothing. Distance takes us.

We move through it until alas

we're all horizon. Time works this

way. Love as many people as

you can. Remember them passing.

———

MY FATHER'S HATS

Sunday mornings I would reach
high into his dark closet while standing
    on a chair and tiptoeing reach
higher, touching, sometimes fumbling
    the soft crowns and imagine
I was in a forest, wind hymning
    through pines, where the musky scent
of rain clinging to damp earth was
    his scent I loved, lingering on
bands, leather, and on the inner silk
    crowns where I would smell his
hair and almost think I was being
    held, or climbing a tree, touching
the yellow fruit, leaves whose scent
    was that of clove in the godsome
air, as now, thinking of his fabulous
    sleep, I stand on this canyon floor
and watch light slowly close
    on water I'm not sure is there.

LATE

As though the far away had already begun

arriving without you, and the evening light

become more gold in its casual longness. That you

were early once means nothing, for the world

in all its sweetness has deposited loss

like glory in the leaves. It weighs upon the light,

gluey, through which you must move, and upon

every living thing, many which have stalled

toward statue. Yet still you go on, knowing

that your arrival could be none the less: The fire

already talling and orange, the rain even now

and hungry. The salt still forming on every

body you touch, kiss, till the song arrives

far beyond the tardiness of any life.

AS

I see a great city, high above a river, on a hill
toward which people are walking. They are carrying
water, and the windows of that city
shine. Their movement seems like a story's
but there's simply no way to tell whether
they're at the beginning or the end of the story
except by the light which keeps changing, or by the weight
of the load they carry. I watch from the woods
near the river. People say I'm still a child
but I've grown older from watching
while the city seems to have grown higher. I met
someone here who claims to have begun the climb
then awoke later, here in the woods. "Why did you
begin?" I asked. "It has to do with the pull
of another season," he said. "People carry the water
to a lake just beyond the city. Often they
drink the water before reaching the lake where it's
stored. One day you too will make—"
but then he disappeared. I wanted to thank him
for building, then leading me through a cage of instants
beyond. Often at night I dream about the city, and the moving
water is like sleep, and the lake, its dull fire, a home.

II

WATER

              Sunlight, brushstroke, sunlight. Worms
in a can, blood on a green sock, and the bluegill, crappie,
and perch all sunstruck.

              —A fish gasping
in the seamless present, and some
gnats now, swirling before them, grainy now.

              And the red cooler
and shiny cans of soda, and apples, all of these now
stuck like balloons, bunched, waving from the past,
reflections still shivering there, the boy
and father fishing beneath the dam.

Then the creaking of chains and gates opening,
and them running, dropping things—tackle box, poles,
stringer of fish as the huge white-bearded spray
pours down around them still slipping on a ledge
now, cutting their shins and hands, slipping through water,
now grabbing at rocks and limbs, adreneline coursing their

bodies back to the car, where they collapse now
with the event still shedding its light like the scar
the sun burned through cloud into the larval
earth and into their brains, all of this, what they recall
half a century later, the heat and joy and wild panic to live.

GO

A small word with no end to it and a wind
that continues into another country.
A word that takes on a different meaning
after someone dies, a word that has a strange
engine that says, "Continue," but then continues
not to move as if burdened with its own
command, a breath which is all exhale. Once
in dream I was sent to the country of GO
with a message for the king who was dying
but seemed to understand, except that he was
unable to reply, then it turned out he
wasn't really a king after all, just a man,
and all the time I was hoping he would say
something like GO FORTH, which sounds kind of
cheery before you start to think about it. The
question now's not so much how to reconstruct
our lives, but how to stop the word that almost gets
to God before it's really gone. The word has
a hollow noise, an otherness beyond. So
what do we do? Does one simply
say, "Now, now," like firing blanks into eternity.

———

WHITE NOTEBOOK

1

In my dream the dead were so many numbers
so I kept counting, counting, and as the shadows
darkened I began singing, till slowly
those numbers began to reappear. I remember how seven
became Mary, how nine became Jim, how fifteen
became William, and how the names didn't end
but kept on echoing, calling out other
names whose syllables blossomed into so many
colors until I couldn't tell which illumined
that room splintered now with light and voices
singing, counting nothing, laughing, remembering.

2

Waking now I watch gold light balloon
through trees and am unsure whether it's morning
or the beginning of the ending of evening
as the building moments secretly compress the joy
and misery of a life into vast granite sheaths
above which the cows and horses dumbly chew.

3

Browsing through a book entitled *Then*, I notice
the pressed wings of so many fathers, mothers, lovers, then
a great wind sweeps through the trees and I see
them haunting the fields like so many seasons, neatly
folding and unfolding the years. Please
tell me if you know how it all goes so quickly.
But look, where those two lovers kissed,

a moment blazed against the sun
till a long shadow fell back and dicotyledonous
leaves lifted ever so slightly our stagnant feet.

4

Looking back through the white notebook, I find a page
where a red spider crawled and you were alive.
Now I write your name again, "Bob." How it stays
put like a toy containing all you did. Look,
I can push it around, amazed
that a life so large could be placed twirling
there. Red dust, green grass, white snow: These you are
arriving toward, disembodied, floating on fire.
How bright you are. How far the poor ladder
of these words. If only in the poem I could spin
your atoms backwards a million times.
Isn't that it? The poem, time's tiny machine?—
till a cloud passes over its own shadow
beneath which white stones and people lie.

POEM

Rolling off our tongues and eyes, does the present

really exist?—as minutes swell into hours, days—

and that dream balloon, years later, rolls leadenly past.

Meanwhile your body's a long road on which I get lost.

I think of you often, but remember most when you

handed me the eraser and empty vase, a potential

emptiness I loved, for what we promise lies somewhat

mysteriously in the past. —Well, you know, as we're all

promised death in the slight wind of a word. When,

when, when, its breeze teases our faces toward a light

we can never quite have, as now, you hand me

this glass of water. Why does its glow seem longer

in evening? The future's a bore where those two

lovers are skeletons whose past was once cells dividing.

Therefore, let me pick thee some long-stemmed dandelions

where we will loiter and marry beneath that beautifully

bloated gold star we call the sun in evening.

—·—

THE WAY THINGS ARE

The violent wonders that contain us. The day
purpling toward cloud—then sun—till the trees
seem defenses against blue and you forget, content
in the now's drizzling lens. Perhaps when we have
nothing to say, when everything is changeless
but changing like waves, perhaps it's then we are
happy, wanting and discussing nothing, as the moment
ripens and goes on till a child asks you a question
you can't answer, and suddenly you remember

one day you'll die. So you get lost in the now, the way
bees rumble their gold chariots through clover
for every bored kid around the pool. And perhaps that's how
some poems come to be, when the days stall
in heat and one is forced to push years into the tedious
hour's piece of paper timed to go off fifty years later
in a library filled with sleep, or in a classroom

locked in rhyme. Perhaps that's why
we delay in order to hurry, creating so many
miniature dramas while the ordinary yawns, and as we
rush toward that tree whose lessening green
gives way to white flowers, already a wild yellow
catches up like shadow, and you arrive out
of breath, dumbfounded at leaves the color of

blood at your feet. Looking back does not help
for the view that was green, voluminous, and sunstruck
seems wobbly and out of focus in a snow
that dreams of our bones and what sugary moments
remain. "I'll take one of those, and one of those,
extra fruit on the side." And why not—that's
what a child does, mouth open like a fish

facing upstream, devouring each moment's
food, or walking in a field, pausing to inspect
glossy things—strawberry, honeysuckle, bee—forgetting
the ouches with wows while opening, marveling,
unfencing the world. The history of a child
is now: Kool-Aid, blood, and flowers, ponds
swarming with frogs, firedogs, and fish.

* * *

It all drifts into the far, the spaces,
while something else like wind arrives, flutters
at our lips, then passes, the undetermined
it that graces being, that white house occasionally
glimpsed which seems to have no walls, yet surrounds
our joys and sorrows. And though we tell ourselves
to make it last, it hovers then vanishes

as our words hover and vanish around what they
name. I say, "The *raspberries* bled in the sun,"
and the barbed word continues to wound
with its music. I step through its rivers, cross its
shadowy, sunlit caves till I'm delivered back
to the knee-high field where the tiny heart still sounds.
I want the word that makes us linger, the laddering hesitancy
that holds for any of it to matter fully, for any of its

shivering to continue. There's the dream
of the house, and then the building, living,
savoring—then there's the leaving and remembering
till all that remains is a picture of the house that's
gone. Now memory becomes a glass of water
containing the light of all surrounding things,
and we drink the water to remember—glad to be here,

glad as the catalpa's green leaves. To make things
last we push them into the far: Reyes and I

felling trees in a picture taken by a friend.
See, we are tiny and will live forever.
Death is close-up and tall. Push it away
with music, poems, laughter, and the sounds
of kids playing by a river. The river lusts

for their laughter, rains with their sun
voices. The river will move them far
and safely into the light. The light that
is the outside we lean to, the light that longs
for us to ripen, the light that graces being,
so that by giving we seem to open time and in
its slow air we linger. Watch the August

bees wrestle gold in purple thistle, watch
them dumb to hours drinking sun from anthers.
Watch them become the sun that is the flower,
all the flowers, fuses to which the bees
are fire, moments moving, both undoing
and doing what's been done, both mirroring
and making. Their fires measure exactly
what they are, what we occasionally

found in song and—while singing—
discovered that the very end of the world
is language, a place once seemingly true
but when we returned to our rooms the words
grew tired, bored, and dusty, elegant
in the shade of things, while all around us
youth leaned lustfully toward that star we call

the sun. We wanted something true
but the truth was something only seen
while looking back, as in a ruined
house we find a truth in splinters and in
rot, the finish and the start. And though vision
is a kind of truth, its time's not yet, and we come
to sadly realize that each moment of our lives

is true but that the whole escapes us. Yet we go
on hurrying, moving to some where through the way
things are, and often, when we get there
we realize there's nothing to do, for the time
like a great sea has not yet, or already
occurred, and we are there alone, standing
beneath clouds, waiting for the moment
to begin, waiting to be caught up to.

———

LADDER

How numbers have become a last world. A man and woman
   hide within the curves of a THREE. How then
is it possible for us to count, add, subtract
   without destroying one another?

In that year I swam in a single pond, often ran
   beside a river in evening until its long
light diminished and was gone.

Animals, their heads bowed toward straw. Sunflowers,
   swallows, bees. Wind, a rustling among grass.
The music of a field, as though from a distance, you
   placed your ear upon a hive.

You gaze and gaze and gaze, till suddenly
   the clouds pull words from your mouth.

The days that move between our words,
   the centuries between our bones.

And would that not be a paradise?—
   When more remains to be told
about an hour than a year?

NO CITY

I open the lake with my body, stroke after stroke
into the chill water, over to the other side and get out
among the blackened pines. Fire, too, is a kind of poem,

for where it begins, nothing more can be said, but the presence
of a poem is a body visible—beyond the senses—through a light
arriving still. And so I walk around, putting little green checks
by the things I love, putting them on the paper
where I hope they will stay

for a while. We gaze
above our tent where the constellations
rise, fish skeletons we've

picked clean of meat. Looking back now on the oasis
of our youth, I think how that new freedom
made an ocean of the moment, just
as in childhood the fever of happiness

spread through a toy. How to recapture it, or the first
touch of flesh, now cloudstuff to bodies
whose hands have plucked joy

and sadness. This afternoon, for a moment, the lake's sheen
seemed to wear our brief
flush of existence. Now looking up, the still

blizzard of stars seems a mythic
house we can't get to. We
are their tired history, their fire
clean in its impossible
distance, unlike what's swept half

this forest. The lessons learned when we were small seem all
but forgotten, and the fires continue to burn
in our country, while this city I've built

out of snow and ash continues to grow. Sometimes in feverish
excitement I touch it, and my sweat
allows its rich past to stick to my fingers. I eat
this way and feed others until no future, no city remains.

—⋅—

WRITTEN ON A PIECE OF BUTCHER PAPER

I think the body writes itself beyond. The calf
sleeps in warm spring light chorused with black-

bird trills. And when I enter your body you
birth me you sing. Stars bleed crystal

into a night sky: Heart, this great sponge
of emotion. It shunts and pulls the days

where a found stone sleeps like a fool's
kiss. I am your fresh slaughter of spring grass,

blue rivers veining the earth. I remember
touching bodies of water, opening

a dress of fire that went on walking before
me and that would never close. Now you are

the sweet, fast darkness of a church where I enter
on a hot day. "Backstraps of loin are best." The customers

couldn't believe it: *I love you* written in lipstick
hanging in the torn air. She was the checkout

girl, he the boy with blood on his apron.

—·—

BLUE

Now they are gathering as they do each October
in the small yellow woods outside their cities,
gathering at dusk to stare at the blue
light only visible now, when leaves are the color
of pears and the clear air feels cold as water
to the touch. They crouch and lean as if toward
ancestral fire, astonished by what they see
or do not, and as they stare the blue light grows
stronger, a blue whose form resembles the moon's
shadowy figures, a blue that in a moment
might crumble and go. Some say the blue light
is what burns on the other side of fire. They would
drink from its ash and listen, the leaded
voice of blue. Here it's their excess that saves
them, that light having mutated their feelings
to what? Some say the blue light's filled
with holes and resembles an animal or god. Larval
the light seems in its becoming, yet a becoming
vanishing toward ends, for when people speak
in the blue light, words blur toward hum. Will they
stay here till the wind tilts sky toward earth,
and snow makes the blue light impossible to see?

YES

On the shore of a lake several people are talking.
They seem lost, not of this world, and the light
is aging all around them. It is snowing and the sun
is out and there are flowers—always, always, always—
while a bird sings through the twilight of three centuries.
One man tells of a spaniel chasing a ball's red curve
over the green earth. "Yes," says another, "how gladly
wild in sun that green," while another speaks of smelling
an infant's head, over and over. "It's a scent," she says,
"like Play-doh mixed with roses." Another man slowly
adds fragrant words to a story as if they were herbs,
then lifts their believable smells up to this world. How
I wish I could smell the wet grass of his hair," says one,
"but talk only cheapens that smell." Nearby several complain
how short the days, and while bee hangs gold from a lily,
others huddle near the shore, stirring a fire with words
toward which the distance burns. The small rain
of their many eyes grieves for a season. They sing
how the closeness of hearts lies in their infinity. The light
continues to age all around them. A farmer tells
how sparrows would ride his cow. How trout would rise
for insects toward clouds. —"Yes, I would like to go back, too,"
another says, "but it's snowing, the sun's out and there are flowers."

—————

III

HEAD OF AN ELK

left for lack of meat, forever detached, familiar
as our lives at birth—or suddenly—now. Then someone
videos it and a city begins: There's a church
of high red worship, an opera of insect voices, a robbery
of smells fabling the day: "Come forward within the city,
across its bridges and walls." —A festival of reds and choiring
browns, yet there are no sounds except that man
in the leaves making love to a woman, and that woman
giving birth, and now that child, his baptism, communion,
and marriage. Sun gongs through the leaves. Mourners
gather around. "I would have given my life for him,"
a mother says, as a priest says, "Have mercy," while flies sing
wild hosannas, and bees rumble the eyes, and someone promises
while another confesses, and someone sells while another
buys, as an army of ants begins dismantling the skull till the sun
—as if glimpsing a body—turns a cloud longish and red.

THE MOUTH

is larger than our lives and always feeding.
Invisible its mandibles, its jaws. The mouth by eating
asks. To it our screams are flowers
flashing their red instants. To it silence
is a gruesome bore in which it drowns. Sing, scream, shout
the mouth says, the mouth that's always
hungry and must feed, the mouth that's a beast
and lover, the mouth that lusts to eat, the mouth
that quivers, the mouth that blows and sucks the moans
from lips, the mouth that loves and asks for loss
while it vomits perfect flowers, or quietly devours
the yellow leaves. *What what what* the mouth wants to know
when you scream, when you shout.
Sing oh please the beauty and lust of the mouth
to stall our slow wonder of being devoured.

RODEO

1

                              A child
we played with was whatever you wanted
him to be. But when we said "tree," he cried,
so we became a silent forest, and he cried
louder. So dark yet hopeful was

our wilderness. Still we like knowing
it's there. A place to go to get covered up
in, to forget, or to conceive ourselves, history
seeking animals. *Sixteen Candles,*

remember that song, marveling at our
youth again. The very trees
could sustain that wish, gently tossing
such precious green, back and forth. —Or

perhaps that we are still
so freshly arrived. —The girl,
fallen in the wheat, trying to reach
the weathered clapboard house that winded

occurs on the horizon. To colonize
means to continually sprawl
order out over the dark, and over the wild,
or as Sir George Peckham of "thys late

undertaken voyage" said, "as pleasing
to almightie God, as profitable to men.
For God did not mean for such souls
to languish amidst an uncleared
wilderness, creeping about in fearsome

2

shadows." Back at the drive-in
gigantic dreamsize faces float across
a depthless stage. The summer
air is warm and sounds of Wiffle balls
and Hula-Hoops. A clean-shaven

father comes to a house where an aproned
mother waits, watches with held breath.
And the dream is so big at times
the house seems empty. —Or maybe it's July
and evening, and kids are buying blue

Popsicles while sprinklers work the sultry
air to green the beautifully false
suburban lawns, as enchanting as
so many gushy whispering trees

to bored and greedy English-sailor eyes.
"For God did create lande, to the end
that it shold by Culture and Husbandrie,
yield things necessary for man's

life." What has that come to mean?
—from times when a slow wagon
got you there, to an electric
now when all the radio towers
loosen their voices and begin to lean

dangerously away from the past.
Someone must be listening, cheering
as the stadiums fill, the schools
empty, and the clock drags us out of

3

nature. In a great midwestern city, that had more rust
than people, I got down on my hands and knees
and prayed to the most constant thing
I knew, the soothing hum

of a generator. I witnessed a great peace transposed
to the landscape of bridges, rapid trains,
and terminals, remembering how as a kid,
looking up through a stripped

engine block, a slant gold light
strayed, gradually purpling down
each sleeve without piston. I gave each one
my hand, and dreamed
of a beauty timed

4

beyond our bodies. Sweet Christ
it's so beautiful, the squared endless acres
ballooning a spun-gold light
as you head west on the Interstates
through Iowa, Nebraska, or Kansas.

An aluminum 16-wheeler, carrying the late sun
on its side, jack-knifes to avoid a car
and sails humpbacked like some fabulous
whale. The great wilderness

5

snores. What felled desire! One summer
men walk clumsily on the moon, only

their breaths heavy as they touch
in slow motion

again and again the ash
body. The toy
flag, whose staff could not be
driven in, recalls

our own wild
impotence—wires to effect
the wind on a place
forbidden because made

6

sacred. The KWIK-STOPs,
the GAS and GOs. Freely we gad
about. Once to know a place was to be
that place. We want so much
to explore, to glide down rivers of print
and down rivers of

film. Our new Don Giovanni's
the man who after 24 hours
sets himself on fire
in the adult video arcade? Does the poor
rodeo of our bodies

7

progress anywhere unexpected? The Angus,
bludgeoned, gaffed, then hung up
to bleed, seemed an apotheosis
of the real. Men in white smocks

gradually took on
robes. Crushed steel led me to this further
carnival of flesh. Now in the church's
organ, I hear the *hummingwhine*

8

of both. Will something please
happen. We're dreaming so very
hard, but there's a fever in the attic
of every house, a dog

barks furiously at our heels, and a sick
man's waiting for a heart.
I think I'll go
shopping. "The best heart

9

money can buy." My wife
tells me I
have beautiful

10

shirts. Wild we
were.

——•——

JOURNAL

That was the year I wrote the one book entirely out of doors,
each of its lines and words among trees or in a field.

I wrote from late afternoon until I could no longer see.
In the perfect unmutilated dark, pages still shone.

I lived alone by the river and had very little—a pencil,
telescope, and hive for bees.

One morning in the fetal light, a white horse and a red one appeared—
one horse white as paper, the other red as blood.

They would feed, heads bowed to the field.

What did it mean as they moved just this side of the trees
unpurpling toward green. Then I watched them disappear.

One became a drift of snow melting, the other a fire dying from blaze.

I watched the sun, its gold light gallop, then slowly rove
through the curves of a skull.

To find there doors and windows gone. —Sunrise, pond, candle.

These are stories begun beyond the body
that can no longer be rescued with hand or glance.

NEW YEAR'S EVE DAY, 1999

I needed something to be completely empty, or something
to be smashed and full.

I needed kindling for a fire,
and there, inside the rotted stump, a wasp's
nest, its paper city exposed. In the body of hive

the brood, a few larvae still wiggling out
among the mummified dead, among the capped and uncapped
cells—so many zeroes—some of them

empty and some of them full. People were beginning
their parties. I would be starting a fire. A winged female
moved sleepily in cold. She seemed to be guarding a proscenium

gone. —Winter mornings, winter evenings, sunrise and sunset
off puddle and glass, the white paint
on the mountains, and the words
between.

The cities, their continuous hum, their sugary lights that dissolve in
     the sun.

I dreamed an X-ray's passionately undissolving milk, not of the body,
but of steel birthing within concrete walls, or of
random acts flitting across screens.

People were coming and going—the young, the old—moving heavily
around windows and doors, for hours, years, until in the first light
their bodies dispersed like feathers,

and the sunlight of a new millennium
fell among buildings and channeled streets
like something within which an invisible key would slide.

And who would turn the key, open the invisible door, and who would be waiting inside?

———

POTTER'S FIELD

And if death is poverty
we are rich now, having finally become

place now, shadowless we are
at peace. News only to earth

now, something to be
still for, over and over again.

So much easier to speak
now, as only wind

resembles our breath
now, as only waves

lap like tongues, our
only reach that of thirsty

green trees. Desire's
ravenous mouth gone

now. What we could not
save cannot be spent

now, though what we
loved remains, red

hearts parachuting,
for we are of earth now

and cannot fall again.

IV

BEFORE US

When the bell rang we all seemed to wake up. Trees
yellowed, blood ran from our ears. First, there
was too much screaming, then everyone was silent,
so we opened people's mouths looking for words.
They all looked the same, though occasionally
we found frozen cries, screams, shouts, still
reticently attacking the air like the leaves
of a red maple. With these we built
a glass city. The sun illumined its walls
and we waited the slow hours of eternity,
the winged filaments of light all our volatility.
So much we wanted to speak, but our
language seemed held in check by another
more painful language's architecture:
a language of loss and of love and of loss.
Seasons sped past. Winter gave green snow.
In spring the grass was red, and summers you
could watch the violet leaves speed toward
autumn's schizophrenia of color. The colors
spoke of forgiveness and our own wild profligate
lives. People said that if you spoke you
would die, but we were already living proof
of the dead, and at every moment you
could see through all of history.

—•—

ELEGY

At each moment the giant deaths and the tiny
births, or is it the other way around? I can never
get it right. If only we could slow the movement down
a bit, then we could see the way hopes are
too early and sorrows too late to matter much to anyone
except the sorrower sorrowing away, always
in evening that song. I remember the man whose two
daughters were killed in a crash. For years
he kept their rooms just as they were—dolls, posters, toys,
while the ship of the world sailed away and he stepped

forever into the perfect coat of his shadow. It seems as we
age everything gets smaller until one day we arrive
to open the door of a tiny house, and there, on the floor,
a feather and a nail, and how we know
a faint wind, or its absence, could create a heaven
or a hell. There's a saying I love: "No matter
where you go, there you are." But there could be
others: Where you were, there you linger. And where you desire,
there you wander and wander in that invisible

green fire. In dream I enter the *Museum of True
Things* and remark on the seeming uselessness
of a BB, a marble, a pin. The guard says, "What can be sold
is constantly changing, and what is constantly changing
cannot be true." It sounded good till I watched
an ocean birth a thousand waves
that held a kind of moving light contained
yet gone, or going everywhere—the wave's perfect
lust for what is, a window where you were
or will be. Chance. We love its ignorant chaos,
perhaps because the man who knew where he was going got lost
in the in between—the heart and loins. I keep looking

for a rent in the fabric where I can crawl out
and see a world stilled, where decisions can be made
without that grey wind blowing papers and people
just beyond their margins. —What? Speak louder, please.
I can barely hear you. Or when the world is asleep
on its long ship I'd like to illusively
enter dreams, saying to each drugged sleeper,
"Look at these irises, touch the moss,
breathe that humus scent, then pull its invisible sponge into your mind
and watch the boy with straw-colored hair run

far into the woods toward home." And you
might ask how these—ephemeral things once remembered—
differ from the immutability of jewels whose past
will not continue to blossom like that trout
shattering a stream's hours, the lavendered-rose
of its sides, the sweet flesh raked from bone, sunlight
through pines—this—the claustral beauty of moments
slipping. The rapture of the fetching present—ants, crimson, shivering
        on
a jay's crushed egg, gnats rising from a river's
moment, or blue gills darting through a pond's dull

glass—this wondrous *now*, so different
from what a fossil tells us. Yes, I think
we grow ancient with the light, craving it more
on the ones we love, the things we own, unrenewable
in springs, except where art stalls the world, throwing visible
stars against the sun, holding a feather in
air, blushing a face with expectation—brush or
words braiding the light so fine it shivers flute, horn,
and trumpet tones, pushing, lifting, easing away
with hardly measurable weight the edging dark.

AS IT HAPPENS

those two people are setting off invisible sparks. They
are moving toward a greater fire, one beyond that of green
blossoming. And the light handling the moment
is undoing itself, not moving, but surrounding, becoming
all things. As it happens these two people are part of the present's
picture, a picture that's shattered over and over, pumping
a long blush upon other people, places.
As it happens there are many sparks that grow
into greater points of light, distant, skeletal, constellating
beyond like the tiny gears of an even greater, invisible
flower where the remembered and unremembered float
like bees. As it happens we are not here long, so we must
choose words that will slowly melt, illumining
dark corners, and remain—faint tracings—in what decays.

———

THREE PANELS

The Light

starts, then the greening, and we
stamen, anther, and fully flower in it. We sweep,
bend, and blow, finding the air. To be
is to fully have the moments, but then they
are gone, the dissolving story we cling to, looking
through its curtains, shaking the dreamy sleepers
who vanish in their rooms. The clouds gold
in a gone light, such that we say, memory
is some light that was. The giving and finding
of light. Bodies over the years moving between
the film of lakes. How long this forever
stalling. Faces glimpsed through clouds on water,
this closeness in distance, and already a remembrance of light
is touching the trees, windows, and houses of an unpeopled world.

A Gift

He walked up to the winter and then into it
with eyes open. He wanted to show how the writing
of snow within snow, of nothing slipping through everything,
shines. He moved among drifts, a pillowed world
where the turns of desire were less dangerous
though no less beautiful in that futureless, indistinct
while. He moved through the individual rooms of snow
as though they were parts of a house where others,
gone, now waited, and he spoke to them through a kind
of steeped sunlight, as the wind blew, and the quick
was tall as it was long, and as he was laying the unsayable
at your feet, you were shy about it at first, then wanted
to polish it and leave, leave nothing, everything, and be gone.

Gone

We would like to speak, but only
wind comes from our mouths. Some gaze
at the sky. Others pick up rocks, looking for words,
while others, and I say this with great sorrow, others
stand in the shadows around objects
they wish to unname. How long it takes
to forget that a bee is a bee, not to notice the gold
hum shivering, pendulous, on a flower. "Close
your eyes now," they say to a child, "and peel the name
off the glance-wounded object like a scab. Now
listen to what's gone and remember the petals'
dizzying vanilla scent all the pushing way up
and how you would call and call and call."

AUTUMN

Why am I so afraid as the cidery smell

of apples lingers in the air? Was it that long ago

I rushed to the wilderness and was married

to the green? Why now do I fear I'll forget my way?

That my wife and daughter won't recognize me? And why

at night does milk vanish from our glasses? Why?

I know that man walking across his roof is safe

because he stands above the heads of sleepy

children. And why do I fear the names of people

will be blown away? Why? Would only that sparrow feed

my eyes, what would I know? Why now do rooms

all smell of clove? And why has my house grown

small? See, I bend to pick it up among the stones.

—•—

VERMEER

Something like a dam of silence
about to break. It's the one where the woman
by a window's weighing pearls. She's holding
a balance, but it's empty, though there's gold—pearls
and stuff on the table. I must have been
twenty when I discovered it in a book on the third floor
of a student house. Everything was so loud: music and fucking
below. So I took the painting into a closet, pulled the metal
chain of the light and sat with the image
on the floor. She's pregnant and her head's tilted toward the light
all over her hands. I had a piece of paper and I needed
to write something, but the quiet wouldn't hold till I put
the foam earplugs in. Were those coins
on the table? And above her head some kind of painting
about heaven and hell. I could hear my blood
surge and the furious noise of my heart, then I began.

THE BOOK

He puts people he loves in the book. He puts
stamps, feathers, flowers. He puts words in the book
he wraps with feelings, smells, and memories.
In the book an old man sings with joy
at the rising of the sun, while a child screams
at the loss of a toy. Earthquakes
occur in the book, while new planets, stars, and black holes
are discovered. In the book the word *is* burgeons
with life, like an anthill in spring, or an ocean
teeming with squid, porpoises, and shad, while the word
was opens into a cave toward the darkening
sea-bottom's floor. Sometimes words in the book
become restless, for example, while he was asleep
the word *now* became a god, a dog, a house, and then a bird
that flew away to another book where it was more happy.
Sometimes it snows in the book and the words disappear
and we build fires in order to stay warm, but secretly
we are making other, stronger words. Sometimes an insect
or a bee lands on a word, mistaking it for a flower.
Sometimes it rains in the book and things grow enormously,
but sometimes things remain unchanged forever, for the book,
though made of moments, seems a wild rest from all that moves.

—•—

A VASE OF CLOUDS FOR MY FATHER

I place their invisible stems in the lake

where they linger, changing frothy face and head

above where we fished, talked below the mountain

whose glacier recalls the day—laughter, blood

on our hands, the present's swift tug and pull

from places we'd loved, lived, the green earth floating

us there, here, changing us, mixing us up with other lives

so we might be changed into what doesn't

or changes so quickly it eludes the hook, shelf, handle,

lifting, folding under, above that light glinting off

water. And there we were, standing in an always evening,

still speaking without voices, looking down into both worlds.

FIVE PANELS

The way a word, feathering air, may outlast a building.
The way desire builds and builds toward nothing.

The scent each April of this and so many other past
beginnings, coming up again, reminding air, lily, iris.

The armfuls of you are never enough. Forsythia's sulphur
shower blooms. —A sleep of bees, then their gold spasm.

All day rain borne down upon the green land till sunlight
opened, climbing the white shoulders of a cumulus.

Sheep graze among flowers and the grass of their pure hunger.
—The oceans whose salt you crave, the city of stars.

———

IT'S TRUE

the dead have left us, but we have
not left them. They are tired of their toys—
stone, cloud, water. They want something
more—to touch a Popsicle melting, to feel
the heat on their faces, or to hold
for a moment the trout's shivering, reckless
glass, a present of the flesh
forgotten while the pillows of their prior sleep
move clouds, or centuries turn like pages
around their motionless hands. We'd like to speak
to them, but the graphs of our words
have long since become bridges of ash
dependent on winds to transport us
to some longing where, cloud-built and yearning
to be filled with a light. But we find them
again in the smell of cut grass, and in
things first seen—the burning stars, from which we,
fragile, hang featherweight tons of memory.

LAST PORTRAIT OF MY FATHER

Blue silk pajamas at 11:00 A.M., the cigarette's
familiar wand, a few Budweiser cans, and the glass
—full gold, bristling foam, light—he sips while talking
through the ten minute video I freeze, then play again, listening,
pushing the cobalt blue, whitening it over the arms, floating
them on the cabin porch against the knotty pine's bright
red trim. Now alongside the collar and buttons, white piping
I line, pulling from blue—that would like to pool—a thin
music beyond violet's aim. Now the hand on his knee, fleshing
the light till fingers hold—nothing, everything. STOP, FREEZE—

rewinding a bit. How to get that smell, trout we'd cleaned,
fleshing their scent, ghosting with viridian the creek smell in.
Now the neck, tapering forward, opening to that face
whose cheeks I puff, now blushing them, mixing madder
with coral, orange. Now the lips, bleaching crimson
to pale rhubarb, half closed on a word, shadow. What was
it? Chalking teeth-light and pulling up the smile.
Lucky here. The mouth's so hard, and eyes—diluting, dissolving
them blue to sky-thin cloud. Now feathering the chestnut-hair,
combing it, hinting the winter-grey where, just above, on
the kitchen window ledge I paint the Palmolive dish soap bottle's
incandescent green, making it three-fourths full again, making
it stay unused, stuck in that now with breakfasty smells. REWIND,

PLAY. Now gilding the Elgin watch—chrome-yellow-gold—
blanching its window face. —And where to place the insect
hands? Now touching up the eyes I hear rushing wind, gushing
creek sounds, so I paint gills on his neck, wings by his hands
as suddenly light volleys from cloud and the small leaf
splits from his head. And what's that by the screen hinge?—
STOP, FREEZE. —A moth, one wing in light, one in shade.

A DISTANCE

And I saw the broken shadows move among trees
and grass. I think they were of people. The light
was saying, "Take each thing and hold its
shivering wonder." Windows tinseled gold, the house
ballooned with light. People gazed at the sun.
"Truth is not a mirror," he said, "but a window
whose glass is gone." We thought long about this
while the house grew smaller against the gaining
darkness. "Here is the key," he said, "but it
bears no relation to what lies behind the door.
All night we moved from room to room,
or perhaps we never moved but only dreamed
till morning lit our wide and empty hands.
We could see the far was near, and something
unlike our bodies blossomed from every door.

POEM TO BE READ AT THE END

In your dream last night the world turned inside out.

Leaves moving yellow toward orange and brown wished to become

viscera. They wanted to exclaim the inside out of things as lived.

It's as though time, too, turned toward a more spacious horizon

less diminished by the presence of carnivalish leaves, a waking

of such into sleep whose colors could only persist in their

parting. And the wind whips a world clean of its flesh

till it appears clear as in the eye of a fish swimming a long way

into a blue stream so wide and fast we call its evening sky.

———

NOTES

"Rodeo": Quotes from Sir George Peckham may be found in *The Roanoke Voyages*, 1584–1590 (London, 1955), 2 vols.

"Potter's Field": Historic burial ground for the unidentified, many of whom were homeless and indigent, located on Hart Island, half a mile east of City Island, NY, NY.

—••—

ACKNOWLEDGMENTS

Many thanks to the editors of the following magazines:

American Poetry Review: "Before Us," "It's True," "Poem," "Song";

American Literary Review: "Late," "You";

American Letters and Commentary: "A Distance";

Boston Review: "Because";

Colorado Review: "Yes";

Denver Quarterly: "Elegy," "Five Desires," "Potter's Field," "White Notebook";

Field: "Passing," "November";

The Georgia Review: "A Glass of Water";

Hotel Amerika: "Autumn";

Interim: "Poem to Be Read Beginning with the End," "Still Life";

The Journal: "Blue," "Rodeo";

Luna: "Memory," "The Book";

Massachusetts Review: "The Mouth";

Many Mountains Moving: "As It Happens";

Mid-American Review: "A Vase of Clouds for My Father";

The New England Review: "Three Panels";

New Letters: "My Father's Hats," "Vermeer";

Orion: "Is";

Pequod: "Last Portrait of My Father," "New Year's Eve Day, 1999";

TriQuarterly: "An Autumn Essay," "The Way Things Are";

Volt: "Head of an Elk."

Electronic Media:

ForPoetry.Com: "Journal";

Poetry Daily: "A Vase of Clouds for My Father," "My Father's Hats."

"Poem" is for Lisa Utrata;

"The Way Things Are" is for Reyes Garcia and George Moore;

"A Vase of Clouds for My Father" was awarded the James Wright Poetry Award from Bowling Green State University;

"Written on a Piece of Butcher Paper" was selected as part of an essay by the same name for inclusion in *Sites of Insight: Essays on Sacred Places,* James Lough, ed. University of Colorado Press, 2003;

"Rodeo," which was originally published in *The Journal,* was also printed in a fine press edition and bound by Tom Parson. It was later chosen for presentation in the Western States Fine Letterpress Exhibit, San Francisco.

Special thanks to John Hobbs, Lisa Utrata, George Moore, Donald Revell, David St. John, Jim Simmerman, all who saw this manuscript in various stages.

Thanks also to Pamela Alexander, Martha Collins, Reyes Garcia, Susan Hahn, W. S. Merwin, David Lazar, and Tom Parson for encouragement, and especially to Steven Huff, Sarah Freligh, and Thom Ward at BOA Editions for advice and encouragement.

ABOUT THE AUTHOR

Born in Faribault, Minnesota, in 1953, Mark Irwin has lived throughout the United States and abroad in France and Italy. His poetry and essays have appeared widely in many literary magazines including *Antaeus*, *The American Poetry Review*, *The Atlantic*, *The Georgia Review*, *The Kenyon Review*, *Paris Review*, *The Nation*, *New England Review*, and *The New Republic*. He has taught at several universities and colleges, including Case Western Reserve, the University of Iowa, Ohio University, the University of Denver, the University of Colorado/Boulder, the University of Nevada, and Colorado College.

The author of four previous collections of poetry—*The Halo of Desire* (Galileo Press, 1987), *Against the Meanwhile* (Wesleyan University Press, 1989), *Quick, Now, Always*, (BOA, 1996), and *White City* (BOA, 2000)— he has also translated two volumes of poetry, one from the French and one from the Romanian. He has received The "Discovery"/*The Nation* Award, three Pushcart Prizes, National Endowment for the Arts and Ohio Art Council Fellowships, two Colorado Council for the Arts fellowships, the James Wright Poetry Award, and fellowships from the Fulbright, Lilly, and Wurlitzer Foundations. He lives with his family in Denver, Colorado, and spends a part of each year in the Collegiate Peaks Wilderness.

BOA EDITIONS, LTD.

AMERICAN POETS CONTINUUM SERIES

No. 1 *The Fuhrer Bunker: A Cycle of Poems in Progress*
W. D. Snodgrass

No. 2 *She*
M. L. Rosenthal

No. 3 *Living With Distance*
Ralph J. Mills, Jr.

No. 4 *Not Just Any Death*
Michael Waters

No. 5 *That Was Then: New and Selected Poems*
Isabella Gardner

No. 6 *Things That Happen Where There Aren't Any People*
William Stafford

No. 7 *The Bridge of Change: Poems 1974–1980*
John Logan

No. 8 *Signatures*
Joseph Stroud

No. 9 *People Live Here: Selected Poems 1949–1983*
Louis Simpson

No. 10 *Yin*
Carolyn Kizer

No. 11 *Duhamel: Ideas of Order in Little Canada*
Bill Tremblay

No. 12 *Seeing It Was So*
Anthony Piccione

No. 13 *Hyam Plutzik: The Collected Poems*

No. 14 *Good Woman: Poems and a Memoir 1969–1980*
Lucille Clifton

No. 15 *Next: New Poems*
Lucille Clifton

No. 16 *Roxa: Voices of the Culver Family*
William B. Patrick

No. 17 *John Logan: The Collected Poems*

No. 18 *Isabella Gardner: The Collected Poems*

No. 19 *The Sunken Lightship*
Peter Makuck

No. 20 *The City in Which I Love You*
Li-Young Lee

No. 21 *Quilting: Poems 1987–1990*
Lucille Clifton

No. 22 *John Logan: The Collected Fiction*

No. 23 *Shenandoah and Other Verse Plays*
Delmore Schwartz

No. 24 *Nobody Lives on Arthur Godfrey Boulevard*
Gerald Costanzo

No. 25 *The Book of Names: New and Selected Poems*
Barton Sutter

No. 26 *Each in His Season*
W. D. Snodgrass

No. 27 *Wordworks: Poems Selected and New*
Richard Kostelanetz

No. 28 *What We Carry*
Dorianne Laux

No. 29 *Red Suitcase*
Naomi Shihab Nye

No. 30 *Song*
Brigit Pegeen Kelly

No. 31 *The Fuehrer Bunker: The Complete Cycle*
W. D. Snodgrass

No. 32 *For the Kingdom*
Anthony Piccione

No. 33 *The Quicken Tree*
Bill Knott

No. 34 *These Upraised Hands*
William B. Patrick

No. 35 *Crazy Horse in Stillness*
William Heyen

No. 36 *Quick, Now, Always*
Mark Irwin

COLOPHON

Bright Hunger, Poems by Mark Irwin,
was set in Goudy by Richard Foerster, York Beach, Maine.
The cover design is by Daphne Poulin-Stofer.
The cover photograph, "Ancient Wasp" by Walt Saeuger,
is courtesy of the National Park Service,
United States Department of the Interior.
Manufacturing was by United Graphics, Inc.,
Mattoon, Illinois.

The publication of this book was made possible in part by the
special support of the following individuals:

J. Christine Wilson & Mary K. Collins
Burch & Louise Craig
Suzanne & Peter Durant
Pat Ford
Dr. Henry & Beverly French
Judy & Dane Gordon
Kip & Deb Hale
Peter & Robin Hursh
Robert & Willy Hursh
Archie & Pat Kutz
Rosemary & Lew Lloyd
John & Barbara Lovenheim
Daniel H. Meyers
Boo Poulin
Deborah Ronnen
Thomas R. Ward
Pat & Michael Wilder

Printed in the USA
CPSIA information can be obtained
at www.ICGtesting.com
LVHW091517080824
787695LV00001B/172

9 781929 918522